MW00596445

Obedience in Finances

By Kenneth E. Hagin

Chapter 1
OBEDIENCE IN FINANCES

My God shall supply all your need according to his riches in glory by Christ Jesus.

— Phil. 4:19

From my experience of almost 50 years of preaching faith, I've concluded that more people fail when it comes to faith for finances than anything else.

The reason is because they're trying to exercise faith for finances, but they haven't planted any seed! They want God to bless their finances even though they haven't planted anything. (Even so, it's amazing how He'll have mercy on them and help them.)

The Bible plainly states, *"GIVE, and it shall be given unto you; good measure, pressed down, and shaken together, and running over, shall men give into your bosom. For with the same measure that ye METE [measure] withal it shall be measured to you again"* (Luke 6:38).

The Bible also plainly says, *"He which SOWETH sparingly shall reap also sparingly; and he which soweth bountifully shall reap also bountifully"* (2 Cor. 9:6). If you want a bountiful crop, you've got to sow bountifully.

You can't reap a crop without sowing seed. You can't go out into your backyard and say, "I'm going to pick some tomatoes" if the ground hasn't been prepared and the seed sown.

You can receive finances through two principal methods:

(1) Believing and obeying the Bible.

(2) A supernatural manifestation of the Holy Spirit.

An example of the second method was that widow in the Old Testament story (1 Kings 17). Her cruse of oil kept pouring out oil, and her meal barrel kept giving out meal — which was just as good as money in those days. That was a supernatural manifestation. *Supernatural manifestations often occur for us in the area of finances because we have obeyed God and have sown seed.*

The first step, then, toward getting your financial needs met is to obey the Bible. God said to Israel:

MALACHI 3:10
10 Bring ye all the tithes into the storehouse, that there may be meat in mine house, and prove me now herewith, saith the Lord of hosts, if I will not open you the windows of heaven, and pour you out a blessing, that there shall not be room enough to receive it.

Actually, we haven't really given until we've paid our tithes.

One fellow said to me, "Brother Hagin, paying tithes — that's just under the Old Testament. That's just under the Mosaic Law. Didn't you know that?"

I would hate to exhibit my ignorance of the Bible by making such a statement. Abraham paid tithes 500 years before the law was given to Moses. Jacob paid tithes 250 years before then.

"Yes," someone said, "but there isn't

any Scripture in the New Testament about paying tithes."

Those folks ought to learn to read. Look at Hebrews 7:8. What about that? That's New Testament, isn't it? *"And here men that die receive tithes; but there he receiveth them, of whom it is witnessed that he liveth."* That's talking about Christ.

God said we were to bring our tithes into the storehouse, and He would open up the windows of heaven. "Prove me now herewith," He said.

But don't do something just because somebody else did it. Don't operate on another person's experience. Operate on what you know the Bible says, and operate on what the Holy Spirit is saying to you.

Once when Kenneth Copeland was here at RHEMA Bible Training Center, he told about the time, back at the beginning of his ministry, when he had an automobile it wasn't too good, so he gave it away, and God gave him a new one.

Some of the RHEMA students, bless their hearts, thought they would get a new car if they did the same thing, so they gave their cars away and walked the rest of the year.

They said, "Well, *he* did it."

"Yes," I said, "but did God tell *you* to do it?"

"Well, no. I just thought I'd get a new car."

"Well, it doesn't work that way."

Because we've got the Bible to follow, I don't need any "leading" to tell me to pay my tithes and give offerings. I know to do that. The Bible tells me that. So go ahead and pay your tithes and give offerings. Often the Spirit of God will direct you to give beyond that.

Jesus said, *"Give, and it shall be given unto you,"* so I don't need any leading to sow. The Bible says, *"He which soweth sparingly shall reap also sparingly."* I just do it. It's when we obey the Spirit of God that things happen.

I'm in my 48th year of ministry. It wouldn't have done me any good 48 years ago if God had told me to give a house away. I didn't have one! And there was a time when it wouldn't have done any good for Him to tell me to give my car away, because I didn't have a car!

Through all these years — virtually half a century — God never told me to give a car or anything like that away. I gave offerings. I sowed seed. I prospered financially.

In the fall of 1981, God spoke to both my wife and me to give a brand new Cadillac away. I already had sold our older Cadillac, so when the Lord spoke to us, I gave our other car, a brand new one, away. I didn't act apart from my wife. She said,

"I got the same leading."

Then, at a seminar I was holding at RHEMA, God told me to give away the airplane that Kenneth Copeland had given our ministry. (It was worth about $160,000 to $170,000.) I gave it to Brother Jerry Savelle.

Some time later, a man I didn't even know (although I'd heard of him), wrote in and said, "We feel led of the Spirit to send you this check for $500,000." That's half a million dollars, glory to God!

I'm well satisfied that if I hadn't obeyed God, that wouldn't have happened, yet I didn't have that in mind when I obeyed God and gave away the automobile and the airplane. I really didn't expect anything in return.

You may think, *I wish something like that would happen to me!* I'll tell you where you've got to start: You've got to start with the nickels, dimes, and quarters.

Chapter 2
OBEDIENCE AND TITHING

A Sunday School teacher in one of the Pentecostal churches I pastored in North Central Texas was a widow woman with five children. She and all the kids would pick cotton for 40 cents a hundred. They lived in a little old house out behind another house.

Yet she'd come by the parsonage on Saturdays and say, "Brother Hagin, we made a few dollars to buy a little food, and here's the tithe. I don't want to wait until tomorrow, because I'll spend it — I know I will — I need it so desperately."

I'd take it, and as she left the parsonage I'd close the door and weep. I knew that I had to take it; otherwise, I would be depriving her of blessing and benefit.

I've had her come by with a dime, saying, "We made a dollar. Here's the dime; here's the tithe."

Her oldest daughter spent seven years in the first grade and never learned to write her name. She never got out of the first grade. Finally the authorities asked her mother not to send her to school anymore — here was a 14 year old playing with 7 year olds. There were no special classes or state schools for retarded children like her in those Depression days.

In church she acted like a 3 or 4 year old; she had about that mentality. If she happened not to be sitting with her Mother and wanted to get up where she was, she would actually get down and scoot along on her stomach under the pews to get up front. Then she would stretch out on the pew like a little kid and go to sleep.

One night during a revival, this girl went up to the altar (nobody asked her to go) and knelt along with the others. She got saved and filled with the Holy Spirit and spoke with other tongues. Instantly there was a drastic change!

Before, she wouldn't bathe. If she got neglected, her appearance would be pitiful. But overnight — the very next night — she came in, sat down, and acted as intelligent as any 18-year-old young lady. Her hair was fixed, she was dressed up, and she looked nice.

We could hardly believe what we saw. Receiving eternal life and the nature of God increased her mentality 90 percent! This was one of the greatest miracles I have ever seen.

It happened at the beginning of World War II. The girl went away to visit some relatives, and while she was there, she acted so nice and looked so nice that a neighboring farm boy asked her for a date. She had never had a date in her life. They began to like each other, and when he asked her to marry him, she took him up on it. After her husband was drafted, she lived with her mother-in-law awhile, and her mother-in-law taught her to read and write.

I left that church to go into the evangelistic field. In the process of time I went back to help the pastor preach the funeral of one of the elderly people. I asked the church secretary, "Whatever happened to that girl?"

She led me outside and said, "You knew that her husband was killed in that truck accident?"

I said, "Yes."

She said, "Well, because of their construction business, he was heavily insured, and she received several hundred thousand dollars of insurance money." She pointed off in the distance and said, "See that housing addition?"

I could see a number of new houses being added to this small town.

The secretary continued, "She is building that addition to the city. She is her own contractor; her own financier. She handles all her own money. Think of it!"

I stood there and wept again — this time a different kind of weeping. I was so glad, praise God, that I had obeyed God and had taken her mother's tithes. This girl had learned to pay tithes, too.

The secretary said, "I'm still secretary of the church. You can count on it, she is on the front pew every Sunday with her two little children. They are the best-dressed, best-mannered children in the church. Her envelope with her tithes and offerings is always there. Every Sunday."

I thought back to where she had come from: Here was a young woman not 30 years old who's building an addition to the city, and when she was 14 years old she had been seven years in the first grade without learning to write her name.

I thought, too, of that Scripture, *"The Spirit of the Lord is upon me, because he hath anointed me to preach the gospel to the poor . . . . "* (Luke 4:18).

Hallelujah, God didn't just single her out and say, "We're going to make an exception out of her." No, the same Gospel belongs to everyone.

What was the difference? Eternal life. The life of God. It was something that came into her that increased her mentality 90 percent. But not only that — she had been planting seed.

She'd been paying her tithes and giving beyond her tithes back when she'd had just a few dollars from her husband's allotment checks. Now she had many dollars, but she still was doing the same thing. Would she ever have gotten to that place if she hadn't been obedient in her finances?

Chapter 3
OBEDIENCE AND HEALING

I was preaching years ago down in East Texas, and when a certain man came up in the healing line, the Spirit of God suddenly moved upon me.

I hadn't been conscious of the least bit of anointing until then; I was just conscious of God's presence. (The Bible teaches that believers shall lay hands on the sick and they shall recover.) In fact, if I had been going by my feelings, I would have had everybody praying for *me*! But, you know, we don't walk by feelings; we walk by faith.

So this fellow stood before me and suddenly the hand of the Lord moved upon me. First I asked him what was wrong with him. He told me that the doctors had said he had a wad of ulcers in his stomach as big as a wasps' nest. They wanted to operate on it. For two years he hadn't had anything to eat but a little baby food, and he couldn't digest that most of the time, he said.

When the hand of the Lord moved upon me, I had my eyes wide open looking at the man. But instead of seeing him, I saw the house where he lived. I described it to him.

I said, "The night before last, you couldn't sleep, but you didn't want to disturb your wife, so at midnight you got up and walked from the front part of the house to the sleeping porch in back." (Down in Texas in years gone by, before we had air-conditioning, we had what we called sleeping porches — screened-in back porches.)

I said, "You had a bed out there, so you fell across that bed, and there you were, holding your stomach — it was burning like fire. Not only that, but your conscience was bothering you, because you belong to this church — you're saved and baptized with the Holy Spirit — but you never have paid your tithes or supported the church."

That fellow looked at me wide-eyed and said, "You must be a fortuneteller or a mind reader — that's exactly what happened!"

I said, "I'm not telling your fortune or reading your mind, either one. I'm ministering by the Spirit of God. In your particular case, before I can minister to you, you're going to have to decide whether you're going to walk in the light God has shed upon your life. What are you going to do about paying tithes and supporting the church?"

He said, "I'm going to do it."

I laid hands on him, and when I did there came another manifestation of the Spirit. I knew by the Holy Spirit — by the word of knowledge — that his body was oppressed by a spirit. (Now, everybody's body isn't, but his was.) I commanded that demon to leave his body in the Name of Jesus. There was no particular manifestation, but I knew it was gone.

I said to him, "Now, you said you haven't had a bite of solid food for two years. Go home and eat a T-bone steak." And he went home and ate a T-bone steak. He went back to the doctors the next day. They x-rayed his stomach and couldn't find a thing wrong with him. Before the week was out, he was back at work.

Somebody said to me, "I don't understand that."

"What is it you don't understand?"

"Well, you ministered to that fellow and told him he didn't pay tithes. He was the third person you ministered to that night, and you never said a word about tithing to the others. Now, if you knew that about him, why didn't you know that about the others?"

I replied, "Well, you see, you just don't carry this gift around with you and operate it as you want to. It is as the Spirit wills."

He said, "Well, how could one get by and one couldn't?"

I said, "Well now, I want to ask you a question: Do you have any children?"

"Oh, yes."

"Well," I said, "how is it that a 4-year-old child can get by with things that a 14-year-old child can't?"

He said, "Because they know more."

I said, "That's why some Christians

can't." Amen. God expects more of some people.

Someone said to me once, "It's not fair that God would expect more of some people."

I said, "Well now, do you expect more of a 4-year-old child than you do a 4-month-old child?"

"Yes."

"Well," I said, "are you being unfair?"

"No."

"The Father God's not being unfair, either," I said.

Thank God for the manifestation of His Spirit. Thank God for the anointing. God in His great mercy and His great goodness condescends to come down to meet men on the level where they are.

Chapter 4
OBEDIENCE AND MIRACLES

Years ago I knew a young evangelist who was just starting out. He was older than I in age, but younger in ministry. He and his wife had five children. His wife's folks were members of my church.

He was off at Christmas and was attending our church with his relatives. I tried to get him to preach, and I would have given him an offering.

This was in 1940. You've got to realize that those were Depression days. We would give a man who preached on a Sunday night $5 in those days. Some will be astonished at that, but I had men in my church whose monthly salaries weren't much. One fellow who worked for the railroad made $37.50 a month. He paid rent, fed his wife and three children, and drove an automobile on $37.50 a month. So, you see, $5 in comparison was good. I would have given it to him, but he wouldn't preach. He said, "Brother Hagin, I'm sort of embarrassed here in front of my kinfolks." So I went ahead and preached.

While I was at the back of the church shaking hands with the people after the service, the Lord said to me, "I want you to give him $10."

"Dear Lord," I said, "I can't give him $10. Don't You know this is Christmas time?"

I could go back and show you my books. I still have them. I was averaging only $43.15 a month for my salary, so $10 was virtually a week's pay.

"Lord," I said, "I haven't even bought my wife a Christmas present yet!"

"I want you to give him $10," the Lord said.

While I was standing there shaking hands with people and smiling, my head and my heart were having a fight. (You don't always know what all's going on inside a fellow!)

Finally I got that $10 together. Nearly everybody had gone home by then, but the young evangelist was standing outside talking to a friend. I shook hands with him and left the money in his hand. I didn't even have a $10 bill to give him. I had to give him dollar bills and change.

Not long afterwards, I heard his mother-in-law telling somebody, "You know, C. was off at Christmas time, and he had just enough to pay his rent and utilities. He didn't have a dime left — not a dime. He couldn't buy the kids anything for Christmas, or even any Christmas dinner. Somebody gave him $10 so they had Christmas dinner."

When I heard the woman, I didn't jump up and down and holler, "That was me! I did it!" No, I just stayed quiet and said, "Thank God. I'm so glad I obeyed God."

A similar thing happened several years later. One Sunday night I was shaking hands with people as they entered the auditorium. Our church was right on the highway, and in those days, before freeways, all the highways went right through town.

A Greyhound bus pulled up and stopped in front of our church. A fellow with a suitcase got off. I recognized him as a minister I had seen at conventions.

I wondered what he was doing getting off at our church like that. It was about time to start church. I greeted him and he told me who he was. I said, "Yes, I know who you are. Evidently you're going to be with us tonight."

"Yes," he replied.

"Well," I said, "preach for us."

While the man was preaching that night, the Lord said to me, "I want you to give him $12.50 out of your pocket."

That doesn't sound like much now, but that was more than a week's salary to me then. I don't know to this day what that fellow preached on — and you know I have a good memory! During his sermon, my head and my heart were having an argument. Just so the preacher would think I was with him, every now and then I'd holler, "Amen" — but I don't know what he said. I was having that fight the whole time he preached.

I said, "Lord, I can't give him any $12.50. I just can't do it! I can't afford to."

I got all the way through that service and still hadn't settled the issue in my mind until we got over in the parsonage. I had invited him to spend the night, and he had accepted. He went to the back bedroom, and my wife went to the kitchen to fix us a bite to eat. I was counting out the money to give the preacher. There were a few dollar bills, but most of the $12.50 was in change — nickels, dimes, and even pennies. (That's the way we got the offering in those days.)

While I was standing there, the Lord said to me so plainly on the inside, "Now, the reason he got off the bus here was because he ran out of money. This is as far as he could go. His wife's down at her parents in such-and-such town in East Texas. Next Sunday he's going to try out for a church at a certain place, and they're going to elect him as pastor."

The preacher came back into the room

where I was. I said, "Hold your hands out." He had to cup his hands to hold that $12.50 in change and bills. He put it in his coat pocket.

Then the devil said to my mind, "Boy, you've missed it. You've made a fool of yourself. You gave away your week's pay." (I had done a little better that week. I had received $17.50 altogether.)

I said to the young minister, "I want to ask you a question: Where are you going?"

"Brother Hagin," he said, "I'm going down to my wife's family. She and the two children are down at her daddy's place in such-and-such town in Texas. I had just enough money to get here. Actually, I went to the bus station, laid my money on the counter, and said, 'This is how much money I've got. How far will it take me?'"

He said, "It brought me here to your town. Ordinarily I would have gotten off down at the bus station, but when I mentioned your church, the bus driver said, 'I go right in front of that church. I'm not supposed to do it, but I'll stop and let you off there.' "

The preacher said, "I don't have a dime left. This is as far as I could go. I planned to hitchhike down to my wife's folks tomorrow. Now with this money, I can buy a bus ticket. Next Sunday I'm supposed to preach over at a certain place (and he named it). I'm trying out for pastor there."

I said, "Brother, that's enough. I want to tell you something. You're the next pastor over there." And sure enough, he was.

About two years after this incident, my wife and I went to minister to a woman who was on her deathbed. Her husband had taken her to three different clinics in Texas. The doctors in each had said the same thing: "We can't do anything. She's too far gone. Among other things, she has an incurable blood disease in the last stages. She's dying. She'll be dead in a few days."

We went into her room to minister to that dear lady. We didn't know her, but one of our members did. We were then pastoring a little old church at Farmersville. As we knelt by this woman's bed, the same voice that had told me to give the one minister $10 and the other $12.50 — that inward voice — said, "Get up and stand up. Don't pray." (I already had my hand on her head and was praying. My wife was kneeling right by me.)

"Don't touch her. Get up and stand up, and say to her, 'The Lord told me to tell you you're healed. Get up.' "

On Thursday she was raised up from her deathbed and on Sunday she was over at our church dancing and shouting the victory!

As we returned home down old Highway 24, rejoicing that God had used us to raise up a woman from the deathbed, just as plainly as if somebody were sitting in the back seat, the Lord said to me, "I couldn't have used you today if you hadn't obeyed Me on that $10 and that $12.50." I'd forgotten it. I had to stop and think, *What do You mean, that $10 and that $12.50?*

"That $10 you gave Brother C. and that $12.50 to So-and-so."

"Yes," I said, "I remember that."

"If you hadn't obeyed Me on that, I couldn't have used you here," the Lord said.

We all want God to use us, don't we? Wouldn't you like God to use you to raise somebody up from a deathbed? How are you going to know it's God telling you to tell them to get up off that deathbed if you don't know when He tells you to give $1 or $5? You see, that's one way you start learning God's voice.

If He can't trust you with $5 or $10, how is He going to trust you to raise somebody up from a deathbed?

What does all this have to do with healing? Everything.

Obedience is the key to receiving from God and it is also the key to being used by God. If we can learn to hear God's voice and to obey Him in the area of our personal finances, it will open the door to further blessings in our own lives and will pave the way for Him to use us in greater ways to bless mankind.